root

melissa tripp

ISBN: 1508983216
ISBN-13: 978-1508983217

dedication

this book is dedicated to anyone i've ever loved or almost loved. you expanded the wisdom of my heart. you made me honest, you keep me honest. you keep me digging— deeper than us. because, does anybody really put their shovel where their mouth is prior to meeting themselves?

even if it wasn't reciprocated, you inadvertently returned me to myself. you inspired me to love harder because you either didn't or couldn't love me enough. you taught me to make masterpieces out of pain. you put my cramped hand on the map.

MELISSA TRIPP / ROOT

CHAPTERS

MELISSA TRIPP / ROOT

preface

born in march of 2015, 'root' is the most important investment i've ever made in myself. writing this book has brought me close to myself in a way that now makes the mundane act of breathing feel light(er). and, living. authentically. i now do without apology or the kind of fear (that consumes). i still get scared. a naturally anxious person, i still worry. i still hesitate. i still question. i still stumble. because, i'll never be immune to the human parts of me. the parts of me that feel intensely fragile yet liberating. my freedom is a derivative of owning the parts of me that are real. every raw phenomena rooted in me— emotionally, mentally, spiritually. past and present. root is me beginning. root is me tying my ends. root is me bridging the gap, having survived everything in the middle. root is the name i give to every calm inside me. my storms, too. root introduces you to me. root introduces me to me. root is the first child i'm raising and watching grow. root is the last breath i'll take and live forever in. root is the book i needed to write.. for me. root is just as much yours as it is mine, now. you give it new pages. you give it new homes. you give it new purpose.

MELISSA TRIPP / ROOT

introduction

here, you will find no structure. no grammatical correctness. no traditional form. what you will find is a voice that can only be audible in this non-distracting and authentic space— an honest voice. a production of truths is the only aesthetic here. my truths, your truths, our truths— our journey. as human beings, as creatives, as thinkers, as learners, as teachers, as lovers, as dreamers.

MELISSA TRIPP / ROOT

1
GENESIS

MELISSA TRIPP / ROOT

do we show the ones

before us "exactly how"

or do we let their demonstrations

be independent findings?

what would be easier?

leading the horse or

shooting the horse?

you see, every journey matters.

every journey needs to happen.

even the stubborn horse's.

don't waste your beautiful mind doing ugly things.

love me so deep that

your roots are mine

and my roots are yours

if only you could see me

the way i see you when

you see me see us.

MELISSA TRIPP / ROOT

sometimes you have

to separate your big

beautiful plan from

small dreamers.

meet me at the great divide

between questions and answers

i know less than i do know

it inspires me

i'm inspired to listen

i surrender my ears

all my senses are the universe's, too

i hear— many things, loud things, quiet things.

i see— many things, vivid things, obscure things.

i feel— many things, warm things, cold things.

i taste— many things, fresh things, dated things.

i smell— many things, hints of things, strengths of things.

i engage all of my senses.

let your inner warrior

come out to play

you have wept oceans

and endured the pressures

equivalent to gravity's stronghold

multiply, dreamer.

subtract, the scared one.

you can win.

scoreboard out of sight, out of mind.

being passionate

about something

doesn't mean

you can't explore

all your talents.

you're never confined

in that way.

don't lose your rhythm now

you've come too far

to slow it all down

you are a breath of cautious

aware and unchained

grounded so admirably

the earth treasures your feet

wind is your ally

gravity, keep closer

blessing in motion.

what better promises than

those that remain unmade?

what you don't make

you can't break

expectations cease

free to make an impression

free to take one's breath away.

you are your word.

MELISSA TRIPP / ROOT

it's not about being deep

it's about knowing what

you're digging for.

put your shovel where

your mouth is.

permit the sun to kiss

your darkest places

blackest burdens

hold hands with the

brightest souls

the moon has reserved

a place for you, too

spread enough light

to inspire the darkness

to get a makeover.

when you speak your mind, you sing your heart.

MELISSA TRIPP / ROOT

your mind satisfies

what your body cannot.

your mind produces waves

your body cannot swim in.

your mind communicates things

your body cannot translate.

the premature thaw
of the frozen heart
teaches us that it teaches
us nothing

the lessons are in the
cold, not warmth

desperation doesn't find you
there
cozy, blanketed, safe
the wisdom doesn't reach you
here
unshaken, unbruised

the lessons are in the
cold, not warmth.

i am not one concept

or many concepts,

i am infinite concepts.

i am constantly

employing new concepts

and terminating old concepts.

i'm constantly becoming.

growing, growing..

until i'm gone.

i am undefined.

i want to crawl

inside your mind,

find a spot in

the furthest corner

to sit, and read

all the thoughts

that shape you.

you must matter most to yourself

in a world where you are easily forgotten

you must travel through the tough terrains

in the direction of self love

pack light— forgiveness,

open mind, open heart, open soul.

MELISSA TRIPP / ROOT

you have feelings
but you more than feel things
in a way that you become them
and they become you

pouring into you
pouring out of you
you emit everything
that touches you

you are deep but you haven't
divorced shallow, either
i don't judge you because
gavels aren't my thing nor
am i qualified to hammer one

the human experience is yours
and you own it so well
i hope you never sell it
never sell out.

i don't have realistic expectations or unambiguous descriptions of beauty. why? beauty isn't clear-cut. beauty is versatile enough to be whatever i want it to be. i have the power to invent my own brand of beautiful. beauty gives me that.

if you could meet anyone

dead or alive

choose your magnitude of potential

even dead, your potential is not dead

it's not really dead

just waiting to be grasped

waiting to be

acknowledged by you

what you think you are capable of

you're only half right

take flight, young do-er, but..

be polite

be on your best behavior

because,

this stranger (your potential)

is no stranger, not to you

your potential knows your oblivion

judge you not, but treat it better

better than that first time you

danced and

abandoned it on the dance floor

if you could meet anyone dead or

alive..

MELISSA TRIPP / ROOT

no such thing as evolving

too slowly or too quickly.

evolve at your own pace.

soul searching has no deadline.

your journey won't always

be a beautiful one.

your journey won't always

be an obvious one.

your journey won't always

be an easy one.

but.

it will be a worthwhile one.

i'm the product of

both the disassembly

and the reassembly of my heart.

MELISSA TRIPP / ROOT

if i can't read your authentic mind,

don't think about me at all.

if i can't listen to your authentic heart,

don't feel for me at all.

if i can't feel your authentic soul,

don't include me in your search at all.

it wasn't until i let

my guard down that

i realized i had been

overpaying for security.

i'm a lover of things.

many things.

things that are simple,

things that are rare,

things that are deep,

things that are quiet.

i've felt you through your chest—

your heart in my hands,

i know what you beat for,

what trembles you.

you inspire me just by breathing.

we're on two

different paths

but we're running

from the same things.

we're

almost there.

MELISSA TRIPP / ROOT

my love for raw wholesome

connections is insatiable.

my lust for familiarity

is containable.

hello,

stranger.

do i have to be close

for you to feel me?

do i have to be speaking

for you to breathe me?

if i am silent, will you

still hear me?

heart exposed,

blanket me.

you are uncertainty.

i want to be in the presence of honest beings, creative beings, seeing beings, healing beings, learning beings, beautiful beings.

my circumstances don't define me,

i redefine them.

MELISSA TRIPP / ROOT

the universe doesn't

prescribe us years

or age to arrive at

wisdom.

experience escorts us there.

plant the seeds you will need

in order to become.

excavate the bad weeds

that aspire to deter you:

people.

thoughts.

habits.

things.

don't be held back.

i remember you

i've written of you before

remember?

you aided the perfect

words in eluding me

you're the write

of my life.

nobody should be given

the option to choose

which parts of you to love.

you deserve to be

loved outright,

every part of you.

all of you.

MELISSA TRIPP / ROOT

if you're going to

be in competition

with anyone,

compete with yesterday's

version of yourself.

i don't choose overthinking,

overthinking chooses me.

MELISSA TRIPP / ROOT

heal yourself before

you reveal yourself.

you can't handle the

whole world falling

in love with you.

you already shine.

the only one dimming

your light is you.

MELISSA TRIPP / ROOT

speak to me in

whispers and screams

everything in between

i don't miss a thing

for your voice is power

i'm in the presence of queen

unprecedented reach

i wouldn't mind you ruling me

but only if you shared the

throne with me, co-reign with me

teach me how to hold my crown

or let me tap into what's innate

you are queen.

i am queen.

but wait.

you are more.

empowerment.

we're staggering against friction

in this moving place

we've exhausted touch with the things

that once hugged our flesh

tighter than knots

our minds are hungry now but

we can't make sense of what doesn't pay

we no longer visit the places that tease us

because.

for us.

the burden's beast is merciless

we can try to forget but it would

only remind us

that when beauty rests

the ugly is woke

desire is

                                                    lost.

nothing lasts

forever but you

will experience

pieces of forever.

i'm a quiet person with loud interior: mind, heart, and soul.

find someone you can build with, not live out clichés with.

note to self:

don't sleep on what's awake inside you.

me and pedestals don't mix.

i make mistakes, let me make those.

i'm human, let me be one.

she whispered soliloquies

i mentally recorded every word

she was the prettiest

little truth teller

off the record.

don't mess with my peace,

i don't like my peace messed with.

MELISSA TRIPP / ROOT

create love, keep love.

she knew her way

but hardly enough

                                        to lead a blind man

                                              to safety

eyes closed the entire time

she saw without seeing

but hey,

she knew everything.

she wore her heart on her sleeve

like most girls do

and like most things she wore

she wore it until she loved it.

with her last breath

she breathed it.

advice to my younger self:

none of it makes sense at first, that comes later. you're going to be tested, and sometimes immense hurt comes with the package. i can almost guarantee it. but, channeled properly, something great can come from it. i know, it doesn't make sense.. again, that comes later. listen.. you'll fly, but you'll fall before you do, and several times. why? wings are not given to you, wings are grown. no matter what happens, don't fill up on resentment. believe in love even when it feels like love is the enemy (it isn't), believe in people even when it feels like everyone lets you down (not everyone will), and believe in yourself even when it feels like your belief in yourself is weakened (you're stronger than you think you are). you can't possibly possess all of the life knowledge that awaits you, now, so don't take the journey for granted.

i'll be seeing you.

writers are slaves to the words they never said.

the only thing

worse than not

being heard is

being heard

and not felt.

love is the magic that surrounds us.

love is the magic in our hearts.

love is the magic in our words.

love is the magic that we must never abuse.

confession:

i used to contemplate writing more than i wrote.

now,

i write as if it were my only mode of transportation.

tell her you love her and she's beautiful.

tell her she's proof miracles happen.

tell her she's the only one.

but only if you mean every word.

start with love.

end with love.

love opens unimaginable doors.

a lot of us get bitter

before we get better.

you too, shall overcome.

once you let the

petty go, it's..

ready.

set.

grow.

if you want to feel the world,

hold hands with a **writer**.

she masters peace, now that's a masterpiece.

.

things money

can't buy is

the motive.

a woman's artistry starts in her mind.

spills into her heart.

blossoms all over her body,

and carries over into her soul.

what to do with love:

give it.

believe it.

feel it.

express it.

make it.

nurture it.

grow in it.

trust it.

cherish it.

protect it.

be it.

you're worth more than

you're willing to believe.

but.

breaking you free is a hostage

situation no one is qualified

to negotiate.

doing things that make you

feel good doesn't make

pain any less real.

it just makes dwelling

on it less of a priority.

when you forgive someone,

you aren't granting them

immunity from the consequences

of abusing you.

you're liberating

yourself by letting go.

rhythm is yours, find your own beat.

sometimes your imagination is all the passport you need.

never leave home without your blessings.

there are no

great loves

without the

love that

originates

from within.

MELISSA TRIPP / ROOT

you're only ever

as lost as your

hunger for

new direction.

MELISSA TRIPP / ROOT

don't lose

your love

for life

lusting for

inanimacy.

a keeper won't

give your heart

away the minute

you take your

gaze away.

MELISSA TRIPP / ROOT

embrace the fellowship

between thoughts

and feelings.

the mind and

heart need not

be adversaries.

physicality only counts for so much.

have you ever feasted on her mind?

immersed yourself in her sea of dreams?

sipped her presence?

not everyone who gets

you is ready and willing

to receive you. not

everyone who is ready

and willing to receive

you gets you.

you don't experience

true liberation until

you reach a point where

you can feel, identify,

articulate, and own your

feelings.

you don't

dictate

for me

what is

and isn't

real to me.

everybody deserves to be somewhere they feel free.

i could fill pages

with the imprint

of your love.

treading amongst those

knee-deep in the hype

of today.

it's true,

i belong to many eras ago.

she longs for

mental feasts.

sadly,

the world

is short on

refreshments.

articulate your heart to me, that's art to me.

everything in my life makes imperfect sense.

MELISSA TRIPP / ROOT

2
SILHOUETTE

i never want to just exist.

i want the universe to breathe

every possible positive human

experience into my life.

MELISSA TRIPP / ROOT

your inner strength

is closer than you

think it is. i pray you

find it, step into your

potential and move

mountains once

you do.

the only way to describe my ambiguous past is to recall feeling like things never stood still. i was hurting more than i was learning. i was falling faster than i was climbing. i was stuck more than i experienced movement. faces didn't match their truths, and places.. most places bore no resemblance to home. i lived in the melody of song and the nursery of words— i still do. does anybody ever truly share in our frequency completely? how/when does someone graduate from seeing through you to seeing you? what you're made of, the true magnetism behind your heart beating, the force behind your soul hijacking your smile every time you mean it, and why each component counts. i'm not so sure i don't still complicate things (connections) with my abstractions and fragmented desires, but..

oh, the wonder years. before i knew it was all part of the equation. before growth had visited my bones. thank you.

i have an interminable

connection with raw space.

completely exposed.

open, honest tones—

without inhibitions.

my artistry is here.

i still write about the parts of myself that

can't be factory reset, with the lights on.

my heart is an ocean of:

birds with one wing.

non-interpretive language.

reversed regret.

eventually.

tall bridges.

skipped beats.

healing.

if the only way you're able to

touch someone is by touching them,

you haven't reached a soul.

MELISSA TRIPP / ROOT

depth excites me.

not the cliché stuff

but everything that

is buried—

the active discovery

approach to mind,

body, heart, and spirit.

relearn your heartbeat. map the colors of every bruise.

pain:

you'll die a thousand times before your heart fails. but, you'll have choices: let it consume you, or use it to make a masterpiece.

it's never the same four walls inside my mind.

you can't expect to find peace

having never entered your own

heart. visit your emotional roots—

stay awhile. explore the freedom of feeling.

MELISSA TRIPP / ROOT

words were the first real friends i ever had.

MELISSA TRIPP / ROOT

i'm a permanent resident of

experiential energy. equal parts

empowering and isolating, these

happenings of substance beyond

the physical realm are what my spirit

is made of. what my spirit lives for.

where my spirit belongs.

MELISSA TRIPP / ROOT

unresolved hurt burrows

itself in every step you

think you're taking until

it immobilizes you.

her heart spoke in incomplete sentences.

MELISSA TRIPP / ROOT

even the most agonizing processes need to be had in order to heal.

i have nothing poetic for you today. there are no words to express how heavy my heart feels— my daddy is gone, and i'm just trying my best to furnish his new home in my heart. i don't know how i'm going to say goodbye, or even where to begin aligning the finality of things with acceptance. but, like the wisest man i've ever known always said: "i'm a TRIPP, and the word 'can't' isn't in our vocabulary." you can rest now, daddy.. i love you.

/wake me up

i remember each time

i tore my heart open.

i've never experienced

anything more honest

than pain.

the easiest way to understand women is to study the sky.

MELISSA TRIPP / ROOT

i want to expose myself

to every richly rooted, raw

element of human design.

MELISSA TRIPP / ROOT

it's okay to admit you're not okay and smiling hurts.

MELISSA TRIPP / ROOT

it's okay to release distractions and explore solitude.

it's okay to fund a calm for your chaos through pause.

it's okay to reserve parts of yourself for only you.

MELISSA TRIPP / ROOT

MELISSA TRIPP / ROOT

I

NOTES FROM MY ANCESTORS

don't believe their books, the ones they'll force
you to carry. your cramped neck and shoulders won't
be a coincidence— we're still hurting and not some
mythical black stains.

we'll fear for you more than you'll wonder about us. for your skin for your skin, for your skin. and we'll be praying for the world you live in where a black woman thinks another black woman is not black enough to be beautiful. *shit is aaall fucked up.*

an honorable black man in a white man's world who'll exhibit the strength of a thousand panthers (even in his last days), your dad's oblique references of his views from the "colored-only" section and riddle-made politics fueled by oppression will be your university as a black woman of mixed heritage searching for her own identity.

you'll contemplate "homemaker" as another name for slavery when you see it written as your grandmother's (who you'll never meet) occupation on your dad's birth certificate.

you'll allow yourself to fill up on love, even when your heart breaks and anger surges through your veins for the mothers of michael and trayvon. there'll be other mothers. and sisters. and daughters, too.

MELISSA TRIPP / ROOT

you won't be so naïve as to allow ideas of being "blind to color" serenade you— they'll remind you. and, you'll embrace it. you'll celebrate it. even when they don't respect it. even when they threaten it. your abundantly loving (white) mom will teach you this.

MELISSA TRIPP / ROOT

there are earths in me i'm still learning to water.

MELISSA TRIPP / ROOT

your world is not a safe

place hiding behind your

chest. you fall asleep with

war on your mind, you

wake up a prisoner of you.

she forgot home when she forgot her heart.

i'm alone with my thoughts, even when i'm not.

i hear you all the time.

and our dog.

and then nothing.

and then i'm reminded.

i hate the years for taking

so much of you from me.

i hated adults for not

explaining where you

were, to me.

that day.. i just thought

you were sleeping.

— reclining chair

MELISSA TRIPP / ROOT

when your shell starts

to crack, which part of

you will be the first to

peer through?

she would give anything to

restore her love for herself.

until, even small talk with

the woman in the mirror

became too painful.

i wanted her to want to connect

with herself on the deepest, truest,

most beautifully strange levels. but,

undeveloped film made her wince.

there are chapters

of her immortalized

in books she's too

scared to pick up.

walk with me where hearts run wild and everything has its place.

give your heart to more real things.

she defeated herself trying to win the love of a ghost.

MELISSA TRIPP / ROOT

i've traveled to some of the

most beautiful places in the

far corners of my mind.

MELISSA TRIPP / ROOT

intellectual poverty is everywhere.

MELISSA TRIPP / ROOT

two hearts, one dialect. let's keep speaking our language.

MELISSA TRIPP / ROOT

i rarely use my mind without consulting with my heart.

MELISSA TRIPP / ROOT

my normal is exclusive to me.

therefore, no one can define

my normal for me. no one can

condemn me for not being

their kind of normal.

the kind of lover i am:

i love consciously.

i love unconditionally.

i love gently.

i love freely.

i love loud.

i love with learning intent.

i love just as intensely as i am loved.

i like my encounters dipped in intellect.

MELISSA TRIPP / ROOT

if i can't speak my heart, i can't give you me.

MELISSA TRIPP / ROOT

love me for me, not who you paint me to be.

if you don't dig me, leave me buried with the love i know.

i live in a different mind zone.

MELISSA TRIPP / ROOT

worst case scenario: becoming a stranger to myself.

there isn't enough room in my closet for your skeletons and mine.

i trust the night more than i trust the day.

MELISSA TRIPP / ROOT

late nights are my playground.

it's when my mind experiences

most of its elasticity, my heart

breathes the deepest, my spirit

its fullest.

MELISSA TRIPP / ROOT

no one knows me better than the phases of the moon.

MELISSA TRIPP / ROOT

waiting rooms.

it's never easy hearing

your name being called.

you're my best friend.

where do i sign up for your pain?

even if it's just for a day.

just so you can feel what it's

like to not hurt.

— when i'm eighty you'll be one-hundred and two

i was raised by my curiosity.

we weren't reaching

for anything in particular,

just something tame enough to

bend to our frame but bigger than us.

i have a night's worth of scars in my heart.

MELISSA TRIPP / ROOT

my soul seeks constant movement— to be spoken to, shaken.

MELISSA TRIPP / ROOT

she left her soul in my pages,

never lifting a pen. she was the

greatest poet i'd ever met.

i don't want you to spell out

the nature of your soul in black

and white to me. let me experience

your grey areas like a beautiful mystery.

MELISSA TRIPP / ROOT

i'm just a mumbling soul who found her bass.

there are waves in me that will not break.

i cry just as much as i smile.

i'm confused just as much as i'm enlightened.

176 MELISSA TRIPP / ROOT

i still look for you in the

buildings that remain.

anywhere you were creates

a comforting sense

of permanence: home.

though.. everything is smaller now,

and nothing remembers my name.

— tunafish, corn chips & iced tea

MELISSA TRIPP / ROOT

3
PULSE

MELISSA TRIPP / ROOT

your soul, an enormous

stadium with a crowd

jamming it packed.

what meeting yourself

for the first time feels like.

learn the difference between

being present in your hurt and

glorifying being broken.

MELISSA TRIPP / ROOT

never minimize your story,

even if it cramps their hands

to carry your book.

MELISSA TRIPP / ROOT

if you can't find it in another person,

give it to yourself. give it to yourself anyway.

do things for you, not for the polished image people have of you. you're allowed to not have it all together. you're allowed to be human. you're allowed to fall into pieces before things fall into place. you're allowed to reject words of optimism when your pain echoes louder. you're allowed to breathe in solitude without having to justify it, even if it means not all familiar faces will be there when you get back. you're allowed to not pack forgiveness— it may be too soon. process. feel. express. don't let anybody navigate your heart's ocean for you.

raise your heart as loud as your voice.

MELISSA TRIPP / ROOT

no two people approach healing the same.

process and let process.

you are what reaches your bones.

shallow is easy.

being truly connected

to what awakens the

fuck out of your soul

takes a unique brand

of courage.

you can only forge

authenticity for so

long before your

insides start to

climb the walls.

MELISSA TRIPP / ROOT

when you hide your heart,

you deprive yourself of

everything it beats for.

MELISSA TRIPP / ROOT

don't let your dreams

disappear building them

only inside your head.

don't take your personal boundaries lightly.

you're the only one who can protect your energy.

just you.

MELISSA TRIPP / ROOT

prioritize a sane space.

and, know that it's okay

to take yourself back from

the things that are spreading

you too thin.

inflicting variations of your pain

onto others won't alleviate yours.

create a space for healing and let

forgiveness tuck you in at night.

don't stand too close to anyone far away from themselves.

loving through the hate

is what gravity feels like.

it's worth every broken bone.

life is one big series of

needing something we

can feel, and being terrified

when we feel too much.

MELISSA TRIPP / ROOT

don't allow your

heart to grow ice

cold letting go of

the things you

couldn't save in

the fire.

make peace with every petal of every flower you've ever wilted.

MELISSA TRIPP / ROOT

you are not safe in your small mind.

MELISSA TRIPP / ROOT

/feel what you say

it's not always about how you say what you say, but rather how you feel what you're saying— really connecting with your words, embracing the power of them. so much is spoken lightly that i wish more people spoke only from the heart.

can we try that?

writing has taught

me my heart—

to speak what is

true for me in

between beats.

MELISSA TRIPP / ROOT

give yourself something real,

something that will carry your

spirit home. connect deeply so

your mind can travel and your

heart can heal.

MELISSA TRIPP / ROOT

you are a powerful framework of

beautiful layers. understand that not

everyone will embrace you with the

intensity and care you deserve.

nurture connections that:

expand your heart.

excite your mind.

capture your spirit.

the biggest protests need to happen in the impassive heart.

MELISSA TRIPP / ROOT

feel everything as deeply

as it hits you, when it hits you.

each time. you're alive now.

be seen for the right reasons.

encourage others to actually

see you, not through you.

be present in your own journey.

the arms of vicarious living aren't

strong enough to hold you forever.

MELISSA TRIPP / ROOT

be honest enough with

yourself to not complicate

your truths with dead words.

reconnect. sit with your

heart in its aching state.

MELISSA TRIPP / ROOT

love deep. the kind that

shakes your entire core

but can't be shaken.

the kind that teleports.

it grows in you, it grows you.

i just want to inspire the kind

of love that hugs the world and

translates easy into other languages.

sometimes my reality checks bounce, sometimes they don't.

one of life's greatest enigmas

is the hostile division between

the lost and those with every

intention of being found.

depth is only cliché to those who play well in the shallow end.

MELISSA TRIPP / ROOT

if i knew what i know, i still wouldn't walk back in time.

MELISSA TRIPP / ROOT

not being able to express yourself is what suffocating feels like.

suffocating is what not being able to express yourself feels like.

MELISSA TRIPP / ROOT

you can't outrun a mind that races.

do today what you're saving for tomorrow.

don't abuse time. it knows where you sleep.

trying to read a woman's mind is a blood sport.

don't confuse ends with new beginnings.

.

MELISSA TRIPP / ROOT

i'm not perfect.

i don't aspire to be perfect.

i don't want to be perfect.

i don't want perfect.

the universe is expanding, expand with it.

count the days until she loves all the things you love about her.

if you have to talk yourself into it, keep out.

i'm not in the business of bad company.

so many feelings, not enough adjectives.

— metaphors

soul searchers are the real treasure hunters.

fill your life with enough love to disarm hate.

MELISSA TRIPP / ROOT

there are just as many things found in translation as there are lost.

i can't vibe with the surface type.

i've got to know that your heart

beats, that your mind moves faster

than your lips, that you're alive.

MELISSA TRIPP / ROOT

giving half of your heart to things is a whole tragedy.

MELISSA TRIPP / ROOT

have your feelings,

show them,

own them.

don't allow anyone to

regulate how you experience

what's real for you and your heart.

you can find home in:

a song.

a film.

a poem.

a painting.

a scent.

a memory.

a season.

a sunset.

a moon phase.

a hug.

a kiss.

give more reverence to

the feeling than the display.

sometimes the compound is

so intense it stains the display.

— a human thing

warm your cold heart, the climate is better here.

you disturb your own peace

trying to segregate the mind

from the heart. find a harmony

between thinking what's real

and feeling what's raw.

don't expect what's

right in front of you

to stay put while you

contemplate

wholeheartedness.

be selfless enough to

set things free.

the discovery of words

birthed me. the imperfect

art of articulation will

probably kill me.

— sincerely, a writer

MELISSA TRIPP / ROOT

embrace happiness with the same intensity as you do sadness.

MELISSA TRIPP / ROOT

connect to her soul before you connect to her bones.

don't let the last time

you allowed yourself

to feel something be

the last time you allow

yourself to feel something.

MELISSA TRIPP / ROOT

pack light for your dark travels.

find space, quiet your mind, turn the world off.

— disconnecting to reconnect

love is like grappling with

the stronghold of gravity

and experiencing the imagined

freedom to fly, all in one.

MELISSA TRIPP / ROOT

MELISSA TRIPP / ROOT

4

ROUGE

i used to hold firm to the belief that "each soul is promised its soulmate." i was also young, naïve, and hopeful. it's where my strength comes from. today, i know that promises are fragile and easily broken. i strongly believe that the eternal connection between two souls is made possible not by the chance of shaping fate, but by the efforts put forth mutually. a little nurturing goes a long way. it has, and it continues to stretch far beyond what either of us could ever have imagined. i've loved prior, you've loved prior, with insignificant manifestations of reciprocity. you've introduced to me, what it feels like to be craved, to be needed. to be enough. as are you. and you're every bit deserving: of my time, of my arms, of my all, of my love.

i love you.

use your pain to expand

your heart, not harden it.

i am everything my heart

has ever bled for and still

echoes like rivers of lost poems.

MELISSA TRIPP / ROOT

home is everywhere.

every soul connection,

every sacred landscape of the mind,

every euphoric stage of the evolving heart—

my spare keys.

positivity:

you're a reflection of the vibrations you harness. each day will require work, mindfulness, embodiment. choose light, always.

there are no secret formulas

to creating a life you love.

be a good person, safeguard

your energy, lead with passion,

make love your theme.

forgive those who walked

away from you when you

needed them to stay. while

you're at it, thank them.

MELISSA TRIPP / ROOT

you happen when solitude happens.

one of the most popular misconceptions about solitude is that everyone who retreats to this unaccompanied space must be suffering or struggling to connect, which isn't always the case. the gentlest of energies fill this specific space: sentimental, reflective, joyful, healing. understand that the practice of solitude is not intended to discourage you from connecting and nurturing real relationships, but instead serves to create a gateway for you to connect with yourself, to nurture a real relationship with yourself. no matter how busy you are with your life, do your best to separate from everything going on around you and enter this zen fulfilling zone.

note to self:

never revoke any fearful bone in your body access to your feet.
move through whatever it is you're afraid of, each time.

you aren't where you used to be. or maybe you are. maybe you're still allowing afflictions to dictate your present and keep you stagnant. maybe you have yet to renew your way of thinking because your heart just isn't there yet— contemplating the alliance of mind and heart a foreign thing to you. and that's okay, you've still got growing to do. shifting in perspective, too. if you're up for it, propel yourself towards a freeing space through the power of positive self talk. create a safe and fluent dialogue within yourself to reinforce your sense of clarity. learn to see things for what they are, not what they used to be or what you wish they'd be. embrace the changes, as hard as that may be and learn what it truly means to grow through what you've gone through. what it feels like, the cessation of war in your bones.

not all stories have heroes.

sometimes, it's you who does the saving.

sometimes, it's you who you save.

love through the hate.

MELISSA TRIPP / ROOT

you'll have to accept that not everything

that accompanies you on your journey is

a permanent fixture. most things,

you'll need to let go of.

healing:

be present in your hurt. the confusion, the uncertainty, the literal
ache. be real enough to pray for your heartbeat.

MELISSA TRIPP / ROOT

I

10 REASONS

WHY YOU SHOULD

BE MORE GENTLE

WITH YOUR

HUMAN DESIGN

one.

you're still learning the continents

heartbreak has spread you across.

two.

you're still exploring depths you never knew about.

three.

you're still clearing house of the wrong guests.

four.

you're still trying to justify wars your mind still fights.

five.

you're still trying to identify the overwhelming void in your soul.

six.

you're still struggling to articulate yourself to you.

seven.

you're still unlearning the paths you've

taken while relearning your feet.

eight.

you're still aspiring to be

beautiful when the magnitude

of your beauty surmounts

a thousand unwritten poems.

nine.

you're still coming alive,

breathing your first real breaths.

MELISSA TRIPP / ROOT

ten.

you're still piecing,

learning to love the remains.

MELISSA TRIPP / ROOT

pain has taught me to appreciate the things that don't hurt.

MELISSA TRIPP / ROOT

understand that not everyone

deserves your vulnerability.

but, it's not about them.

it's about you and refining

your human textures.

self love:

like a tree, you will experience high winds and hard rains. but. know
that you are built for it. give your storms names. become.

celebrate your healing journey.

the ability to gracefully

embrace what's painfully

real for you is your magic.

know when to retreat inside of yourself.

for yourself.

MELISSA TRIPP / ROOT

strength is embracing

every real thing happening

inside of you. every storm,

every calm in between.

it makes you connected.

alive, free.

landscape your inner beauty. mirrors won't always tell the truth.

/on caring too much

no such weakness, you've been wronged by myth. wrap your heart around the empowering transformation of being invested.

MELISSA TRIPP / ROOT

a woman's heart is one of the most divine forces in the universe.

MELISSA TRIPP / ROOT

leading by authenticity

generates powerful waves

of honesty and vulnerability.

peace is yours to find

on your own terms, at

your own pace. with your

own hands, in your own

home. your soul cavity,

yours to fill.

sometimes it takes growing apart

to grow your parts. move closer

to yourself. you deserve to feel your

branches extend beyond the clouds.

MELISSA TRIPP / ROOT

in order to trust,

understand that

trust is something

you will be constantly

building, and repairing.

trust is always evolving.

MELISSA TRIPP / ROOT

your spirit is too important not to protect your energy.

you are a humble tree. do not let a budding ego disturb your seeds.

love your hardest.

you deserve every

gift this wholehearted

surrender has for you.

home is where the heart doubles in size, and beats like a poet's.

i never truly understood clarity

of heart until i started making

peace with everything that broke it.

it's a beautiful thing to live

your truths free from the

cage you put yourself in.

i have an elephantine hunger for learning.

and the flexibility to unlearn.

the real heroes are

those who have saved

themselves from themselves.

external riches can never fund the forces within.

seek to understand before you seek to be understood.

i've done some of my best life

gardening work in comfort-free zones.

have you stepped outside of yours lately?

don't feed the robot. be human instead.

MELISSA TRIPP / ROOT

be comfortable with who

you are, even if it makes

others uncomfortable.

MELISSA TRIPP / ROOT

you're beautiful because you love you.

MELISSA TRIPP / ROOT

never forfeit your character for a false sense of reputation.

liberate your mind,

think things for yourself,

and think them through.

spend more time with your thoughts.

there's real currency in that.

the most beautiful people are always the last to know.

MELISSA TRIPP / ROOT

get excited about life.

anticipate the unknown,

cozy up to the familiar.

whether you start with

the new or revisit the old..

just, be happy.

if you're going to define something,

leave a little room to redefine it.

true generosity doesn't keep a tally.

MELISSA TRIPP / ROOT

learning is the only thing you can't finish once you've started.

believe in something that believes in you.

MELISSA TRIPP / ROOT

what grows you knows you.

MELISSA TRIPP / ROOT

you are not someone's

boxed perception of you.

celebrate every eclectic

sound your heartbeat is

made of, every layer,

every truth.

wander deeper into every beautiful experience.

adjust your grip on beauty as you encounter it—

fleeting phenomenon. taste the proof.

MELISSA TRIPP / ROOT

don't let anyone define

your purpose for you.

whatever it is that creates

a raging fire in the pit of

your soul, go with that.

MELISSA TRIPP / ROOT

my heart broke so i could be here:

learning.

growing.

teaching.

healing.

MELISSA TRIPP / ROOT

pedestals aren't for people.

MELISSA TRIPP / ROOT

humans. reluctant to grow in love.

it's easier to crush your petals than

it is to explore your bleeding roots.

MELISSA TRIPP / ROOT

sometimes the most

beautiful part of a

woman is the very

ground she walks on.

forgiveness is freedom. when you forgive someone, you're freeing yourself from the confines of what that person did to you so you're able to move again, and on. they may care, they may not. that's just it.. forgiveness frees you from the madness of the need to know.

5

THE SHE FILES

my encounters with women,

my encounters with myself,

our encounters with ourselves.

note to women:

be good to your heart. don't toy with hearts. protect your hearts. but, don't deprive your hearts. grow them the size of the moon until the same light exudes from you. project your transgressive energies with caution. there are young women learning from you. and, mothers. there are mothers waiting for you to make them proud, to make yourself proud. impress yourself— the right votes will count.

she spoke from a place of not yet

healed, not entirely broken.

she craved more than she could devour.

she tried to rebuild every bridge she

had burned, never realizing that the starting

and ending points would never be the same.

she occupied your mind like a

prelude to a riot worth dying for.

MELISSA TRIPP / ROOT

she was every breath you tried to take but couldn't.

she was the first language i spoke.

MELISSA TRIPP / ROOT

she was a river of haunted memories and fleeting loves.

she left something to be traveled about her, and

i never knew how to appropriately pack.

MELISSA TRIPP / ROOT

her heart spoke so loud through her

chest it bruised her ribs. she still muffles

her ears and is still tender to the touch.

MELISSA TRIPP / ROOT

she longed to return to her naïve skin. back

to before she was old enough to drive any lessons

home. to relive every compassionate caress.

she was beautiful but stuck aspiring to be beautiful.

she never learned to hold her own hand.

she could feel her lungs filling up with

everything you ever said but never meant.

she was bruised in places she never accessed to heal.

i wish i could have met her at her absolute core.

she had to learn to trust the ground beneath her feet

before she could correct her sense of direction.

she left her shadow with

immovable ghosts from her past.

she retreated indoors on sunny days

instead of getting it back.

your mind's hell is heaven to her heart.

MELISSA TRIPP / ROOT

her heart was etched in the fleeting

sunset hues and every tide she tried to

swim against. she loved as deep as the ocean.

she never stuck around long enough to let the nectars of being authentically present stick to her insides.

she missed the way words felt

from people who meant them.

her spirit still dances the same songs.

and, she won't stop rehearsing long enough

to feel the true bass inside of her.

she broke every bone in her

body trying to make room for

the things that didn't belong.

her heart was so cold she'd never

survive a night inside of herself.

MELISSA TRIPP / ROOT

she was the kind of woman you could sit and talk with in the dark. until, she became every monster who hurt her.

she was half contemplating what it

would feel like to forget, half subconsciously

watering the tree she grew of memories.

she's the poem i can only write in the dark.

light never traveled through her.

MELISSA TRIPP / ROOT

she was everything she was aspiring to become, she just couldn't see it. things like needed, wanted, loved.

she was the flower whose petals never showed their face.

MELISSA TRIPP / ROOT

she lived vicariously through the superficial lens of others,

having never explored the magnitude of her own beauty.

she could never tame her lust for

the idea of love. it became her solace,

never tasting what hearts are made of.

she never understood that getting out of her own way was half the journey. i wonder if she still hinders every step.

she never looked more beautiful than she did

the night she peeled back her layers. there was

something present and conclusive in her eyes.

she wasn't afraid of anything,

until it came to embracing herself in

a real and honest way. she never

learned to be vulnerable.

she was like a vast ocean—

full of meaning,

preludes to storms,

and incalculable allure.

MELISSA TRIPP / ROOT

she never wanted enough for herself. eventually,

she deprived herself of everything.

MELISSA TRIPP / ROOT

she was the safest and scariest place to hide.

she painted herself the colors others wanted her to be.

until, she realized she owned her canvas and no one else.

she was a stranger to herself. until, she started looking

for herself outside of the safety of others.

MELISSA TRIPP / ROOT

she took stock in having everything left to give.

even in its fragility and impotent wisdom, i'd never

seen a heart beat so beautifully.

she left her heart open despite all

the doors slammed shut in her face.

she persisted in love, growing her

heart the size of the moon.

MELISSA TRIPP / ROOT

before you fall in love with a writer, understand that every chapter must matter. you cannot confine a writer to your territorial/reactive impulses. even the past has the potential to become art framed by a pen. it is the way we as writers navigate. please, find a way to be okay with that. don't hold our compasses (words) against us. it is possible to live just as deeply in a writer's heart as we live in our minds. we're just as present in our hearts. just, sometimes.. our imagination is the only passport we have. only you know if you want to board separate jets. but know this.. no one can love you as consciously or as freely as a writer. no one sees you like a writer sees you. you are already poetry waiting to be written. feel the world, hold my hand. tight.

MELISSA TRIPP / ROOT

I

snippets of letters i'll never send

i want to go back to the days where the only thing i feared was what was under my bed, not the women in it.

WARM-UP

i wasn't prepared for the intensity of the impulses that came packaged with you— pseudo-committing myself to someone for the first time. what did i know? you were seasoned, and i was just starting out. you lost your patience with me more than you were patient with me. you talked sense to me when nothing made sense to me. you were there for me, you were safe to me. you wanted the best for me, even if and when it wasn't you. you branded me then let me fly.

AMATEUR HOUR

my wounds from the first woman to break my heart were still fresh. and you still had disruptive tenants living in your heart, too. while our ideas about our love were full of hope and promise, we were kidding ourselves. we were just kids ourselves. by the time the complexities of our young love caught up with us, we were already moving on.

GAME PLAYER

you anchored me so deep i forgot the name of my ship. only, we never made it to sea. i left you at the same shallow shores i met you. i don't miss you, nor the fantasy you created. we're much older now. i let you go with the last tears i cried for you. the only thing i feel is sad for you. and, i pray for the first 'real' conversation you have with you.

LATE BLOOM

you were unexpected. you were a new light for me. you gave me
something to look forward to, something i could plan for. i taught
you things, you showed me things, we never made a mess of things.
you redefined fun for me. even when it got tricky, we always found
a way. until, growth got in our way.

FILL-IN

you weren't supposed to get hurt, you were my friend through all those nights you listened to me hurting. you weren't supposed to fall for me, you knew i wasn't prepared to catch you. you weren't supposed to capture my heart, you knew my heart was still hers. i never meant to be so unfair.

FRIEND ZONE

you were more than a friend to my friend. it was too late to apologize, and i wasn't sorry. i'm just sorry i didn't see karma sprint back around. you never bought my "just a friend" card, and i never bought yours. our trust was doomed from the start.

BAGGAGE CLAIM

i cared for you, even when it got me into trouble— unwritten rules never applied to us. but, you wanted a family with me that could never be mine. because, you decided i didn't deserve the truth. i hope, now, you're playing house fair.

once upon a pedestal, no one could touch you. you touched me without ever touching me. gripping my soul even before you were given the slightest clue what you meant to me. i accepted your feelings not being immediately reciprocated (in that way)— you were in pain, and i loved you enough to not make it about me. you needed me to be your friend, and i was. without hesitation. evolving into what we became took time. it wasn't always easy, but you made it okay. we laughed together, we cried together, we laughed through the tears together. i could be myself with you, even when you made me nervous. when you hurt, i hurt, and vice versa. eventually, your heart was ready and you gave it to me. i was ready for you, i always ready for you. but, we only complicated things. we were this complicated thing. and when it all went wrong, i just wanted my friend back.

CAKE BOSS

we connected on some of the deepest, most intimate levels. but, you wanted the comfort of familiarity with her plus the excitement of starting something new with me. that was uncomfortable, no matter how mature i tried to be about things. you never bothered to draw any lines to know which ones not to cross— you didn't respect me enough. you saw me but you never saw me through.

i met you at the cusp of meeting myself.

who were we?

MELISSA TRIPP / ROOT

MELISSA TRIPP / ROOT

6

AFIRMATII

MELISSA TRIPP / ROOT

I

being:

notes on authenticity

there are ancient cities in me that
are still visible through the ruins.

i gave my heart for this.

MELISSA TRIPP / ROOT

challenge yourself to reconnect.

fear binds us to one another just as much as it keeps us disconnected. from ourselves, too. the things you're running from are the same things making you crawl inside of yourself trying to find a grip and keep it there.. to eventually make the climb— the pyramids of intense feeling. you cower from deciphering the things worth holding onto from the things that aren't meant to stay with you. because, contaminating your soil means growth never comes. and you're okay with that. you're safe here. complacent and not having to face the light because you're comfortable in the dark. you've taught yourself to satisfy the echoes of your pain so that you don't have to give it a voice. you've convinced yourself that love is the enemy so you overpay for protection. you ignore the beautiful so that you don't have to acknowledge the ugly, too. understand.. that.. you're depriving your hungry heart of a raw chance. and, i pray that one day you can meet yourself behind the façade.

MELISSA TRIPP / ROOT

have more authentic conversations with yourself.

if you aren't being exactly

who you are because you're

afraid of the response, you're

letting them cage you. you're

letting them erase you.

MELISSA TRIPP / ROOT

celebrate your transparency— stay open.

the flowers growing inside your afflicted

heart will thrive even when the sun

disappears for awhile.

honest eyes are an infinite source of wisdom.

MELISSA TRIPP / ROOT

i only genuinely began to

expose myself to happiness

once i started connecting to

more of what's real. what hurt,

what still hurts— healing.

those who condemn you

for expressing exactly what's

written in your heart are afraid

of real things. you're the real thing.

MELISSA TRIPP / ROOT

don't just articulate the parts

of yourself that are easy.

articulate the parts that scare

you, too. make it real.

tell me a true story.

MELISSA TRIPP / ROOT

search your soul and keep everything you find.

in order to maximize your

relationship with yourself,

it needs to be real. connect

your core. feel. travel your

truths with only a backpack.

the culture of false connections keeps us distant from ourselves.

MELISSA TRIPP / ROOT

II

doing:

notes on ability

MELISSA TRIPP / ROOT

overcoming the "easier said than done" syndrome:

far too often we discourage ourselves from things before we've even had the chance to convert our intentions into action. we convince ourselves that we're incapable of making any real progress because either a) we don't know where/how to start or b) we're too afraid to start. the key is to not allow ourselves to become immobilized by negative thinking and fear by using the following techniques:

1. **step out of your comfort zone.** it is here where we discover new strengths and develop a better understanding of our weaknesses.

2. **believe in yourself.** while it's human nature to seek outside validation, understand that you're the most valuable support system you'll ever have.

3. **set realistic goals.** it's important to remember that your journey is exclusive to you— authentic goal setting should take priority over competing with/catching up to anyone. start small, start with what's in front of you (what you can reach) to build momentum.

4. **stop sabotaging yourself.** *(see steps 1-3).*

MELISSA TRIPP / ROOT

we sever our minds

with the sharp edges

of mediocrity and

complacency.

you have to learn to quiet your mind before you can trust it.

MELISSA TRIPP / ROOT

i'm a master of nothing, a student of everything.

you've come this far.

don't reverse your steps

for any reason other than

to reflect— find the blessing

in every scrape, bruise, scar.

you're not entitled to anything you haven't earned.

note to self: your best is good enough.

MELISSA TRIPP / ROOT

be about the growth you

wish to see. break unhealthy

patterns, eliminate negative

influences, prioritize your

passions, stay focused.

some of the best

advice i've ever

received came

from listening

to my instincts.

MELISSA TRIPP / ROOT

what doesn't kill you,

builds in you. you don't

become stronger until

you turn that pain and

those hardships into

blessings.

MELISSA TRIPP / ROOT

III

seeing:

notes on self love

MELISSA TRIPP / ROOT

why i stopped hyphenating "self love".

the use of hyphens in "self love" has been resonating on a strange level of irony for me, lately. love is just as much an individual phenomenon as it is a universal one, yet i feel we don't create enough space for it inside. we don't allow it to radiate independent of social acceptability and our desire to be loved by others, enough. we tend to be great at meeting others' needs, thus neglecting ourselves and making it that much harder to return to the empowered place where we feel worthy (without validation).

removing the hyphen, for me, represents the space required to actively honor new and old commitments to ourselves not attached to anyone or anything. space to be better to our hearts. space to love our bodies. space to learn to say "no" when too many "yes"s deprive us of ourselves. space to not allow ourselves to be mistreated. space to find our voices and to never lose them once we've found them. space to tell our stories. space to start over. space to make our own choices. space to sit with our real selves beyond our surface selves. space to express. space to redefine inner feelings of peace. space to heal. space to grow.

MELISSA TRIPP / ROOT

make peace with the parts of yourself

that are not easy to love. you're still

learning your roots and how to stop the rain.

MELISSA TRIPP / ROOT

embrace yourself before you can't face yourself.

MELISSA TRIPP / ROOT

no one should ever feel like they're entitled to mistreat you.

love thoroughly. yourself, too.

understand that self love is grown

completely independent from even

the most prosperous relationships.

get in tune with yourself.

your deepest self, your

truest self. the one who

is most vulnerable. the

one who masks.

she/he/they is love.

when you self invest, you make an asset out of yourself.

your bests and worsts make you the masterpiece you are.

honor yourself enough to let go of the

worth others have determined for you.

MELISSA TRIPP / ROOT

MELISSA TRIPP / ROOT

IV

making:

notes on creativity

dear creators:

there will be times when the forces of perceived creative obligation will compel you to try to be everything to everyone. you find yourself utilizing your unique gifts in ways that render you too accessible. consequently, you have less and less room to breathe. you don't want to disappoint those who look forward to and generously support your work but you're struggling to keep good balance. while your artistry sits inside of you, you've never felt more outside of yourself. you're in silent crisis. pushed and pulled. you just want to find your way back: to before the expectations, to simpler times, to you. know that reclaiming this seemingly fleeting space is as easy as you make it— start with stopping. yes, pause. but not just any pause: guilt-free pause— pause for clarity, pause for reconnecting (with you), pause for sanity, pause for growth. take all the pause you need. those who truly support you will not only understand but encourage it.

sincerely,

choose yourself before you lose yourself.

MELISSA TRIPP / ROOT

no such thing as too

big a dream. trial and

error is meant to grow

you, not discourage you.

MELISSA TRIPP / ROOT

whatever your art is, keep following it.

i have a mind full of ideas and a vertigo of free reign.

MELISSA TRIPP / ROOT

don't limit your art to other

people's expectations for it.

go against the grain, expand

beyond your comfort zone,

find freedom in creating.

if you have a dream,

raise it like a child.

be firm yet gentle.

preserve the love.

art heals.

art builds bridges.

art teaches.

art grows us.

art keeps us honest.

art connects us.

art introduces us to ourselves.

art saves.

every dream needs a starting point.

excuses are the anatomy of sabotaging them.

passion:

the thing that moves earths in you, orbits you,

keeps you up at night with its deafening truth telling.

V

having:

---

notes on relationships

MELISSA TRIPP / ROOT

love vs. being in love.

in order to explain love below the surface, you have to have scratched. while each journey is exclusive, it's important to note that the shared nature of love's truths apply to all of us. like, the difference between love and being in love.

love: a solitary force.

love thrives on its own two feet independent from the investment of relationships. in its abundance, we're able to explore love's mechanics in abstract proportions without any concrete commitment or definable reasons— we simply love. our intents are pure and there's nothing intricate about it. it engulfs us but doesn't weigh a pound— it isn't heavy. as a stand-alone, love is light. like water.. fluid.

being in love: implication of romance, attachment, absoluteness.

we've all been there, we're all there— in love. unsolicited dictation of the heart, mind, body, and every fiber in our spirit. we all have our own versions of what being in love looks like, but the variances of what being in love feels like are few and far between. indescribable feelings.. but, we still try. because, we believe in the merit of romance, the metaphoric photograph of two souls completely bound and what that looks like, and the possibilities of having your efforts and passion matched. to build or not to build.

those who genuinely want

to know your heart are worth

being open with. they are tender

with your intensity, and care what

you're made of.

MELISSA TRIPP / ROOT

love is a beautiful thing in the right arms.

there are two kinds of people:

the kind you invest in,

and the kind you don't.

MELISSA TRIPP / ROOT

to limit intimacy to one

dimension is to have yet

to explore true closeness.

resolve your

internal conflict

before you start

a war in someone

else's heart.

MELISSA TRIPP / ROOT

expectations are venomous.

MELISSA TRIPP / ROOT

you can't have a

real relationship

with anyone you

can't have a real

conversation with.

if you allow every painful experience of having your full heart met with empty arms define you, it will. understand that the only way to heal is through vulnerability. you need this space to recalibrate your reality— integrating responsibility for your own happiness into intentful action. you need this space to love better. are you brave enough to show your scars?

you can't teach anyone how

to love you. you can only

declare your worth and be

mindful of what you allow.

MELISSA TRIPP / ROOT

7
JOURNAL

MELISSA TRIPP / ROOT

i lose most of the wars being fought inside of me. the same wars i continue to fund with my heart. just to feel. i don't always know which battles are worth fighting. and the battles i do win, somehow still feel like losing. some days, i smile and mean it. other days, i smile purely because hope needs a face. there are even days when i don't feel like picking my weapons up. i often have these silly ideas about preparing for an abstract hero i know is never coming. because, this is where i save myself. this is where i hang onto every notion about beauty and scars being connected.

/the reality of healing

THE KEY TO EMERGING FROM THE AFTERMATH OF UNEXPECTED STORMS THAT INTRODUCE CHAOS INTO YOUR LIFE IS LEARNING TO MANIFEST YOUR PERSONAL POWER— FINDING CLARITY IN THE AWARENESS OF *EVERY THOUGHT, EVERY FEELING, EVERY SENSATION*: FROM THE PLEASANT TO THOSE THAT BROUGHT ON THE HEARTBREAK. UNDERSTAND THAT IT IS NOT THE PAIN THAT DEFINES YOU BUT RATHER HOW YOU CHOOSE TO CHANNEL YOUR PAIN THAT DOES. LET IT GO. BUT.. ON YOUR OWN TERMS. ON YOUR OWN TIME. IN YOUR OWN SPACE. FORGIVE THOSE THAT NEED FORGIVING (FOR YOU, NOT THEM). RELEASE WHAT NEEDS RELEASING TO FREE YOURSELF FROM WHATEVER HAS TAKEN YOUR INSIDES HOSTAGE. MAKE PEACE WITH THE PIECES YOU HAVE FOUND, THE PIECES YOU HAVE YET TO FIND, AND THE PIECES YOU WILL NEVER GET BACK.

MUCH PEACE.

MELISSA TRIPP / ROOT

MELISSA TRIPP / ROOT

MELISSA TRIPP / ROOT

MELISSA TRIPP / ROOT

MELISSA TRIPP / ROOT

MELISSA TRIPP / ROOT

MELISSA TRIPP / ROOT

MELISSA TRIPP / ROOT

MELISSA TRIPP / ROOT

MELISSA TRIPP / ROOT

MELISSA TRIPP / ROOT

MELISSA TRIPP / ROOT

MELISSA TRIPP / ROOT

MELISSA TRIPP / ROOT

MELISSA TRIPP / ROOT

MELISSA TRIPP / ROOT

MELISSA TRIPP / ROOT

MELISSA TRIPP / ROOT

MELISSA TRIPP / ROOT

MELISSA TRIPP / ROOT

MELISSA TRIPP / ROOT

MELISSA TRIPP / ROOT

MELISSA TRIPP / ROOT

MELISSA TRIPP / ROOT

MELISSA TRIPP / ROOT

MELISSA TRIPP / ROOT

MELISSA TRIPP / ROOT

MELISSA TRIPP / ROOT

MELISSA TRIPP / ROOT

MELISSA TRIPP / ROOT

MELISSA TRIPP / ROOT

MELISSA TRIPP / ROOT

MELISSA TRIPP / ROOT

MELISSA TRIPP / ROOT

MELISSA TRIPP / ROOT

MELISSA TRIPP / ROOT

MELISSA TRIPP / ROOT

MELISSA TRIPP / ROOT

Made in the USA
Lexington, KY
29 May 2017